SHORT STORIES

FOR SENIORS

Collection of 101 Inspirational Short Reads, Short Romance Stories, Senior Moments, and Bedtime Stories for Adults

JACOB MAXWELL

"Keep reading. It's one of the most marvelous adventures that anyone can have."

Lloyd Alexander

TABLE OF CONTENTS

INTRODUCTION 11
CHAPTER 1: REFLECTIONS ON YOUTH 12
TOAST OUR BREAD 12
ALL RISE 13
CATCH THE ROACH 14
TREE CLIMBING SPREE 15
GREEN LIFE 16
TIME CAPSULE 17
FARE IS FAIR 18
WATER TRICKS 19
MONOCHROME LIFE 20
FRUIT AND VEGGIES 21
OLD SCHOOL 22
CAMELIA'S TEETH: I 23
BABY FOLLOWERS 24
GRAND GOATS 25
BRACELET BUDDIES 26
MOOD RINGS 27
PAPERWEIGHTS 28
A WITCH'S FIRST POTION 29
LAUNDRY DAY 30

BATCH OF '72 31
HAIR CUTS 32
PIANO PLANS 33
THE MASON JAR 34
CHAPTER 2: LOVE AND RELATIONSHIPS ... 35
LOVE BLOOMS 35
CANINE CARE 36
THINGS TO DO 37
TAN SNOWMAN 38
PRETENSE PERFORMANCE 39
MIRROR FRIENDS 40
VEG TO VEGAN 41
THE SECOND TOOTHBRUSH 42
FRUIT SANDWICH 43
PHOTO SECRECY 44
NAME GAME 45
CAKE DECORATE 46
PET CALL 47
LOVE AT FIRST CRASH 48
SIBLING THINGS 49
HOME SUPPORT 50
THE SAFE BET 51

DARTS AND CARDS 52
GRAY HAIRS 53
THE GO-TO GIFT 54
STAR STORIES 55
CABLE COMPLIANCE 56
YARN LOVE 57
SAND RACER 58
PAINT PRINTS 59
FOSTER POWER 60
CHAPTER 3: JOURNEY AND ADVENTURES 61
LINGUA FRANCA 61
MUGGY DAYS 62
STAR-STUDDED DREAMS 63
CAMELIA'S TEETH: II 64
SMILE IN SOLITUDE 65
WHALE OF A TIME 66
QUEST THROUGH TOWN 67
THE SOLO TRIP 68
CRACKER PLANTS 69
CAMELIA'S TEETH: III 70
THE MOVIE GANG 71
SKYDIVING 72

GOLDEN SAND 73
WAITING.. 74
SALTY AND SWEATY 75
HEARING HELP 76
ECCENTRIC TASTE 77
THE GARDEN MAZE 78
SWIMMING SOCIALITES 79
NIGHT LIGHTS 80
CHAPTER 4: HUMOR AND LAUGHTER 81
PAPER PROGRESS 81
HEIR'S HAIR CONCERNS 82
REAL PLASTIC 83
BANK ON DAD 84
NUMBER STUMBLE 85
SALTY SLEEPER....................................... 86
CONTACT LOST 87
CHANGE FOR NONE 88
SKY'S THE LIMIT 89
OPPOSITE DAY 90
WINDOW ALERT 91
THE RIGHT ANSWER 92
NO MORE DOOR 93

HUM, SOME MORE 94
GREEN ROOM 95
SHOCKING POWER 96
PAINT WITH POLISH 97
HAUNTED LABS 98
BEE IN YOUR BONNET 99
STICKY SITUATION 100
BATTERIES 101
SUGAR AND BACON 102
THE GIGGLE TRAIL 103
CHAPTER 5: LESSONS LEARNED 104
TRUST IN ME 104
POWER 105
PATIENCE 106
BOOK NOOK 107
THE BEST DIVORCE 108
SMART LUCK 109
CAMELIA'S TEETH: IV 110
HELPERS 111
WINNER 112
PRIDE 113
UNPARALLELED PARKER 114

RUN LIKE A GIRL 115
CAMELIA'S TEETH: V 116
BOUQUET TOSS 117
PERSPECTIVE 118
FLOWER FORMAT 119
ACAPELLA BURP 120
ADHD AT 80 121
HEIRLOOM HANDOVER 122
PAUL'S PH.D 123
THE THIRD SIDE 124
PASSION 125
CONCLUSION 127
REFERENCES 128

INTRODUCTION

Gather the kids, gather the fam; it's time to read some pleasant stories and jam! We're back with *Short Stories for Seniors*, a book brimming with 116 funny and gentle tales for the whole family. These are real-life stories centered on the gentle, defiant, and quirky nature of growing up and growing old. Let's not be hindered by age but instead be bolstered by it.

If you find these stories familiar, it's possibly because you relate to the people or the situation to an extent. Find your hook and let these stories engage your silliness and sensibilities.

So, sit back and relax, or reenergize your sleeping wit! It's never too late to yoink out a megaphone from behind your rocking chair and spread laughter and smiles around the neighborhood.

CHAPTER I

REFLECTIONS ON YOUTH

TOAST OUR BREAD

When Joanie's dad was little, he'd love to raise his bread and give a toast. You read that right; he thought "bread" was what people used when toasting achievements.

Frankly, you can sympathize with his misunderstanding. But even after his parents explained it to him, he held fast to the idea of having bread for any important night. He taught my mom, all my siblings, and me about the idea of giving a toast with a slice of bread.

Now, anytime Joanie's kids visit, he eagerly hands out the slices. They'd have tea parties with elaborate toasts using plain bread. At the least, it discouraged drinking within the family and also proved that his dadly sense of humor had been running strong since the sixties.

ALL RISE

Demi and Lyall's grandma was a civil court judge. When they were little, they'd enact court cases complete with the accused, witnesses, jury, and a judge.

Sometimes, they'd get Grandma in on it. She always said it was her favorite part of the visit when she had to listen to her granddaughter explain to the jury of stuffed toys why the Sharpie was not responsible for keying her doll's car.

Even better would be her grandson accusing the Sharpie of defacing their older sister's doors with stars and scribbles.

But the best part was when her grandkids acknowledged her decisions and always called her "Your Honor" and stood up when she was on her feet. Apparently, they were better behaved than some of the attorneys she'd come across in her career.

CATCH THE ROACH

The free period before lunch gave some students time to work on their assignments. Cliques of cheerleaders, sporty kids, and asocial ones were spread out in the space. They'd managed to stretch all their papers out over two tables and were the loudest. The librarian had to keep shushing them.

And then they saw the cockroach.

One girl screamed, and everyone jumped and scattered about, trying to spot and kill the roach. The quarterback stepped forward to do his civic duty to crush the insect beneath his size nine sneakers. But before he could even try, the quiet kid leaped up and landed on it with her Crocs. Everyone peered in to get a good look at the stain left on the floor.

"Oh, come on!" the quarterback complained, but the others just burst out laughing. When the librarian finally kicked them out, they were still in high moods, slapping the girl on the back and nodding in respect. Nothing like killing a cockroach to make new friends.

TREE CLIMBING SPREE

Little Martha would often climb the meandering mango trees in the backyard. The rough bark was perfect for her grip, and the tough branches could easily hold her weight.

She'd skitter up the trunk like a monkey and perch herself ten feet off the ground, legs swinging happily. Without books, phones, and gaming devices, she still managed to entertain herself for hours.

Twenty years later, Martha found it hard to believe she'd swing from the trees, scraping her tender palms from the cracked and rough bark. Red ants populated the branches and leaves now. She didn't dare step too close to them. But a few days of nostalgia and longing were enough to try. She sprayed water over the ants and shooed them away from one of the lower branches, thick enough to support her heavy weight.

Martha used a stepstool to reach and sit on the branch, swinging her legs like the precocious child she'd once been. The childish delight was gone, but the touch of joy would last a lifetime.

GREEN LIFE

Simran was raised to be very earth-conscious. Her parents were one of the first in the neighborhood to separate their trash into dry, wet, and plastic—an ongoing system for a while now.

When she was five, the family had been invited to a baby shower. Her parents had boasted about Simran's ability to clean her own plate. She eagerly demonstrated it to the people at the party and received keen applause. The other kids at the shower flocked toward her and began following her around.

The father-to-be had cheerfully offered the kids extra candy. Simran diligently unwrapped the treat, threw the candy into the trash, and stood there in the backyard staring at the wrapper. The children followed her actions and were very pleased with themselves despite the laughter.

Decades later, Simran was often told this story any time she spoke of her quaint little job in a flower nursery. It's not the highly coveted role of an afforestation regime, but Simran was always one to take small steps toward a greener planet.

TIME CAPSULE

The minute she'd retired, Meiying had reworked her old backyard into a blossoming garden.

She'd been digging near the trellis when her spade caught the rough side of a metal object buried in the mud. Meiying frowned and tugged out a small box. It wasn't locked, but the lid was tightly wedged. She grunted and yanked the thing open.

Oh.

Oh my. The small box had a floppy disk. She hadn't seen that in a long time! Beside it were an envelope, old coins, friendship bracelets made of twine, and an old photo of a puppy. Meiying caressed the photograph. Her little puppy brought teary memories to the surface.

She could barely remember her ten-year-old self writing a letter to a future version of Meiying. But she read the letter, grinning at all her astronaut dreams. Well, soccer coach was close enough, eh? The floppy disk was a mystery until she found a PC that could accept it.

What's life without a little mystery? Meiying was quite happy with hers.

FARE IS FAIR

For the past twenty years, Gordon would wait near the bus stop with bags of coats, scarves, and winter boots for the homeless population that stayed around the area. His wife, Jennifer, was always supportive and asked him one day about the reason behind it.

In 2003, he'd scored an interview for a graveyard shift as security. When he'd reached the bus stop, it was 10 p.m., and Gordon had missed the last bus. Some taxis lingered around, but he didn't have enough cash on him.

The drivers refused to lower the price for him due to his unkempt looks. That's when he saw a girl in frayed clothing. Desperate, he approached her carefully and asked for spare cash.

She was probably frightened. But she gave him the money. He got to the interview on time and was hired.

"I wait near the stop every year for her," Gordon told his wife. "I really think she was homeless. I want to pay her back."

Jennifer went along with him this time.

WATER TRICKS

Tony's house had hard water sources, and every few months, the taps, showerheads, and sprinklers would be blocked by salt crusted around the spouts. To figure out a way to clean them, he asked his grandpa, Joe.

"So, you want to reduce the tap-fixing bills?" Grandpa asked.

"It takes a lot to clean out the hard salts. Do you know a trick?"

Grandpa sterilized a safety pin. He used the white-hot metal point to dig through the salt crust in one of the taps. Tony did the same for all the spouts in the house. It took an hour, but he managed to clean out some of the salt. He tested the tap, and to his surprise, the water burst out with full strength.

"How'd you know, Grandpa?!" Tony asked eagerly.

"The Navy is a ripe old place for learning all kinds of shortcuts," Grandpa smiled. "We used our compasses to clean out salt crust near the windows. Shall I tell you the time we used fire extinguishers to cool our drinks?"

MONOCHROME LIFE

Jeanie never hit an artist's block. It hit her. She'd been painting for the better part of 50 years and was used to the ups and downs of inspiration. But this was the worst she'd faced. None of her visuals made sense, and she simply couldn't find the wherewithal to try something new.

She sat in front of half-finished canvasses, unable to muster the will to complete any of her works-in-progress. It reminded her of her grandkids, who'd abandon their doodling to spend time with her. Jeanie smiled, remembering them watching old movies from "black-and-white times," as they'd say.

She paused. Those words conjured up an image. That's it! She'd draw a black-and-white scene!

Jeanie dug out pieces of coal from the old fireplace and grabbed a new sheet of paper. Warm-up sketches took time, but now, she needed this. Using the charcoal, she let her hand fly across the paper, sketching snow-covered mountain tops and a blinding moon over a dark backdrop of inky sky. Jeanie grinned. Moments like these made her humble profession worth it.

FRUIT AND VEGGIES

When Kiara was little, she hated fruit and vegetables. They never suited her picky palette, and this annoyed her mother.

"They're healthy for you! You need to eat them in between all that junk food, you hog!" her mom complained.

But Kiara couldn't stomach it. Apples had an oddly wet sugar taste, mangoes were slimy and changeable, carrots were too sweet, and tomatoes left a vile taste! Everything put peculiar visuals in her head and made her averse to them.

The neighbor sympathized with Kiara's predicament. She cut an apple into cubes and sprinkled pepper and salt over them. Kiara closed her eyes, pinched her nose, and munched on a piece.

It wasn't the weird sweetness but had a balanced taste.

"Plants tend to have a natural sugar that some kids simply don't vibe with," the neighbor informed her. "So experiment with your food, kiddo."

Even in her sixties, Kiara hated the regular taste of fruit and vegetables. But she would gladly eat cucumber with molasses, green mangoes with salt, and bananas with chocolate syrup.

OLD SCHOOL

Jenson visited the court once a month. Basketball had been his burgeoning career and his life right up until retirement and subsequent joint pains. He couldn't dribble across the court anymore but gained a lot of joy by spinning the ball on the tips of his fingers.

Sometimes, he'd meet up with a few pals from old teams and spend the day on the court. Soft games with less running and more simple shots were the focus. They reminisced about their glory days and recognized that while those days were in the past, the memories still kept them going. Jenson had always been and will always be a basketball player. That's where most of the happiness and satisfaction sprung from in his life. He had no regrets about the way he managed the games.

When Jenson watched the new kids play the game, he compared their style to his own from back in the day. It had changed, but the passion remained the same. He couldn't wait to see where the kids would take the game.

CAMELIA'S TEETH: I

Two milk teeth persisted in her mouth. They were nearly as stubborn as Camelia. She was in her mid-40s and could now see a clear difference in the tiny baby teeth compared to the rest of her permanent teeth.

Camelia had grown up with rather naturally straight-seeming teeth, so her parents didn't get her braces. Her permanent incisors never descended, and her milk teeth did all the work.

She'd grown out of her fear of imperfect teeth as she'd become older. Now she loved seeing a new dentist react to this. Most were professionals and just nodded. But one of them had actually paused long enough for her to tell him, "Yes, I still have two deciduous teeth. The head dentist said I'm better off keeping them until they develop actual problems."

It was fun watching experts learning stuff about her to keep up. The dentist replied, "Dope. Aside from those, your teeth look pretty good."

"They have a habit of developing cavities when I'm not looking. I might be back in a few months."

"See you then, Camelia."

BABY FOLLOWERS

Beatrice's grandfather was the baby whisperer. He had the knack of knowing what any baby seemed to want at the moment. He'd told Beatrice, "Watch what a baby does for at least 20 minutes. Do they like extra attention? Do they want to be left alone with their toys? Or do they prefer to be with just one or two people? Make use of what interests them."

For example, Beatrice's cousin just had her first birthday party with the family. Grandpa Andy watched the little tyke devour her cake before crawling around the house in her diaper. He sat right by the cake with a magazine because the baby always went back to it. He would just smile at her and resume reading his tabloid. The baby grew curious about this old man who sat next to her cake but didn't steal it away from her.

The baby followed him around for days. Beatrice assumed that the baby saw him as the cake protector. Grandpa Andy had successfully wrangled a new follower.

GRAND GOATS

Jason grew up on farmland. He loved the chickens and ducks and was curious about the goats. One day, the smallest goat kid headbutted him hard enough that he fell back.

He wasn't eager about farm life. His family always said his strong skull was not right for office jobs, but he'd prove them wrong. Jason took a business economics course in college, eager for a job to get him out of the small town. Surprisingly, he learned more than the curriculum.

The things he learned helped him see a better way to improve farm life. He could rearrange the space between the sheds, get more animals like pigs and fish, figure out how to balance poultry and produce, and even hire more hands to help. He actually had a good sense of business acumen.

Decades down the line, when the family's farm was flourishing beyond his expectations, Jason loved to invite his grandkids over for long summer stays. Of course, he routinely had to yank them away from the goat shed lest they get headbutted.

BRACELET BUDDIES

Stephanie was seven when she received a bracelet-making kit with colorful plastic beads and strings. She checked them out for a week before abandoning the set.

When her two grandkids found the box decades later, she happily gave it to them. But history repeated when both kids fiddled with the beads before abandoning the kit in favor of a video game.

"Don't you want to try them, Anna?" Stephanie asked.

"Eh," Anna shrugged. "They're boring, Grammy."

Stephanie's father had gifted the kit to her with his hard-earned money. Instead of making gorgeous bracelets and necklaces for herself and her friends, she'd given up.

To make things right, Stephanie sat down and began to string the beads up. She varied the shapes and designs, building lovely patterns for both bracelets. Once ready, she tossed them over to the kids.

"Whoa! Grammy, you made this?!" Jerry exclaimed.

Sheer elation filled her heart as Stephanie watched her father's gift put to good use. She received several pieces of wayward jewelry, and she treasured them all.

MOOD RINGS

Chris found a mood ring in one of the older stores in town. It looked exactly like the one he'd had in the 1970s. Nostalgia bowled him over as he gawked at the lovely ring in its little case behind the glass wall.

The store owner offered him the case, and Chris checked the band. "Is it sterling silver?"

"Absolutely, sir! This is one of the originals from Reynolds and Ambats' first set!"

Chris doubted that. Most mood rings simply didn't last beyond five years. The one he'd had remained with him for a decade, but by then, the color had no longer changed.

On their own, rings held a lot of bias. Most people bought them for others. Whether for love, affection, or platonic doting, it was just rare for people to get jewelry for themselves. But mood rings were the excuse people used to buy for themselves. And Chris admired this one.

"I'll take it," he nodded, unable to stop grinning. Time to see if 21st-century rings failed as badly as the 20th-century ones!

PAPERWEIGHTS

Siblings Mac, Judith, and Sally were back in their old home, reminiscing about their childhood.

Mac was four when his dad actively parented for the first time. Mom had gone back to the office, and Dad—since his job let him stay at home—would try bizarre tricks to occupy the kids so he could work without interruptions. Sometimes, he'd hide their toys and give them hats to pretend to be detectives and search the house. He'd even leave the sleeping babies on top of his stack of documents so they could stay close by and act as paperweights.

Dad's quirky behavior encouraged Mac, Judith, and Sally to run their households similarly. Each of them had their offbeat mode of handling chores, taxes, and stuff about life. But the similarities resided in the way they included their families in the work they did whether it was practicing for a conference meeting or helping their kids with homework. In their experience, it was better to manage a hectic life without separating the work and home aspects too much.

A WITCH'S FIRST POTION

Mabel was blessed to live for decades outside of city life. But her children resided in the city. When Mabel had to leave the cottage and move in with her daughter, she had a great deal of separation anxiety.

It was a warm fall day. Mabel took a break from her packing and looked out into her garden. An idea struck her, and she gathered her bucket and filled it halfway with water. She picked up fallen leaves, plucked flowers and petals, and dropped them all into the water. She found thc perfect stick to stir this mysterious solution. Digging through the mud with the stick, she added clumps of it into the water to turn it dark and dirty.

Mabel couldn't help but laugh. As a little girl, she'd tried similar things, dancing around the garden and pretending to be a witch or a fairy. It had been a long time since she'd made a magical potion, but it gave her the same joy as it had in her childhood.

LAUNDRY DAY

Ruth spent the first few decades of her life without a washer and a dryer. After all, how could a pair of machines clean clothes better than human hands? Then her daughter bought them and was quick to stop Ruth from berating her.

"Ma, this makes things a lot easier and faster!" she said excitedly. "The dirty clothes go in this drum. It washes the whole load, and I transfer it to the dryer. Watch it spin!"

"Proper drying needs to be done outdoors!" Ruth persisted. "Not inside a loud box."

"But instead of spending hours every week washing the clothes, linen, curtains, covers, toys, and a bunch of other things, I can relax," her daughter replied. "It's a great investment, Ma. And look at the dryer."

The drum spun and tumbled the clothes so fast Ruth went dizzy. When it stopped and beeped, her daughter brought it all out, and Ruth felt the warmth of the clothes seep into the air and calm her down immediately.

"See, Ma? I look forward to laundry day now."

BATCH OF '72

Leo's class had commissioned T-shirts when they graduated. Unfortunately, the tees looked foolish with black squiggly lines on a pale grey background.

When Leo heard about the alumni gathering in 2019, he went for it. He hadn't attended the past meetings but had a sense of longing for it now.

The schoolyard was crowded with people from several decades. Leo wandered for a while before he spotted that ugly gray T-shirt.

BATCH OF 1972: ROCK 'N ROLL!

The man in it was balding with grey hair above his ears. Leo approached him eagerly, and they got to talking. Soon, they located two other men wearing the same T-shirt! Others from various grades also recalled the goofs of 1972 with their silly tees. Leo was amazed.

After a long time of no contact, he left the alumni meeting with no less than seven new numbers. They made plans to keep in touch, and Leo decided to search his house for the gray T-shirt. He wanted to surprise his new-old friends the next time they met.

HAIR CUTS

Madison always cuts Chester's hair. He'd never gone to a barber. Ever since they were married, she was the only one wielding scissors around his head.

This was evident when she'd gone out of the city to visit friends. An important meeting at his work was scheduled at the last minute, and Chester's hair was a little overgrown and a lot unkempt. He used pomade to smoothen the longest strands down, but it gave him a scrunched-up look.

The meeting went well enough, and when he was back, Madison had just reached home. She looked at his hair and burst into giggles. "Chester! Do you go out like that?!"

He sighed. "The humidity hit the pomade hard. Everything was sticking up by the time I reached the office."

"Why didn't you just trim a bit off the sides?"

Chester shrugged. "Sorry, honey. My hair is yours. I have no business cutting it."

Madison just chuckled and brought out the scissors. They'd been going strong for 35 years and knew they'd be the same for another 35.

PIANO PLANS

Music was life. Bruce had it all planned. He could already play the piano well, so all he had to do was post a few original pieces online, go viral, and earn big bucks. Easy.

When that didn't happen, Bruce was the only one surprised.

"You can't expect success overnight," his father advised. "Many famous creators were well into life before their careers became lucrative. Tolkien published the first book of The Lord of the Rings when he was 62. James Horner was 40 when he composed for Titanic. You've to keep at it for years, if not decades. But don't do this because you're expecting outrageous success. Do it because you love it, and it loves you back enough to keep you afloat. Think you can manage that, son?"

Bruce exhaled. "Yeah! I'm going to be playing the piano on my 100th birthday, that's for sure!"

When he turned 83, he played the piano as he did every birthday and knew he'd do it for several more years. "Barely famous but happy" was Bruce's motto.

THE MASON JAR

Donald had just moved into a nursing home. It was hard to leave his home of 32 years, but he simply couldn't stay there on his own.

When he unpacked in his new room, a mason jar filled with folded pieces of paper awaited him. Whoa! Don remembered this graduation gift from classmates to classmates several decades ago. Everyone taped their name to their jars before going around writing small messages of thanks or hope for each other.

Donald sat back to read them all.

Some were funny. "What d'you call a cross between a joke and a rhetorical question?"

Others were sweet. "The past four years were great! Hope to run into you soon. I know you'll always make the best of what life hands you, no matter where you go, Donnie!"

Don chuckled and laughed and cried, reading all the notes. When he was done, he packed them all and placed the mason jar right on the nightstand. He figured he'd need them for the hard days.

CHAPTER 2

LOVE AND RELATIONSHIPS

LOVE BLOOMS

Ellie's grandparents had a peculiar first meeting in the 1960s. Grandpa worked in construction, and Grandma's family hired his company to build a garden with a fountain in front of their house.

Every morning, when the workers arrived with their tools and worked in the yard, Grandma would rush over to the window to watch them discreetly. Eventually, she mustered up the courage to bring them lemonade and food.

Grandpa thought she was interested in them and leaped at the chance to ask her out when they were nearing the end of the contract. The garden was coming in beautifully, and she agreed.

Fast-forward four decades, Grandma revealed why she'd approached the workers. Grandpa was the only one who'd taken good care of her begonias all through the construction. He still helps with her garden now.

CANINE CARE

I remember when my grandpa's vision went bad. He was 82 and insisted that his eyes were fine, all the while bumping into the table and shed, spilling papers and gardening tools constantly. He refused to visit the doctor, preferring to squint and feel the walls.

My mom got a job offer in the city. Without her during the day, Grandpa was even more likely to fall, so we commiserated and adopted a dog. No one was more excited than me, and nobody was grumpier than Grandpa.

He ignored the two-year-old canine who'd just grown into her paws and loved to leap around like a prized stallion. But in a few days, Grandpa offered treats, scratched her back, and grudgingly accepted her. By the weekend, our dog happily led Grandpa all around the house, yipping if he got too close to tables, walls, and doors.

He'd gone for an eye check-up and got diagnosed with mild cataracts. Once we sorted that, he'd watch over the dog with as much love and attention as she gave him.

THINGS TO DO

For John's 30th birthday, his sister gifted him a book titled *50 Things You Must Do Before You're 30*. He didn't share his sister's sense of humor.

It was maddening that these books had expiration dates on one's accomplishments before they were middle-aged! John had done only one of the things listed in the book: spend a whole day in bed. He could try that again soon.

But what if he wanted to fly a kite at 31? Would he be a failure if he even tried it?

John had a sensible enough self-esteem, he thought. He didn't need to be disappointed for not visiting Bali. He was a satisfied, single man living in his cozy bachelor pad. Romantic relationships were not a priority. He had a good support system between his friends and his family, whom he reached out to when they needed help. His salary was optimal, and he loved his job.

Perhaps the right thing is: there is no pressing list. John was kind and happy. Life was good.

TAN SNOWMAN

It was just past Christmas when Nana woke up and saw that her shelves had been raided. Some of the bottles were pushed to the side, and her sunblock lotion was missing.

She didn't fuss about it. Who needed sunblock on a snowing winter day? But Dad later found the culprit and was beside himself with laughter.

The youngest grandchildren woke up early and found the snow outside appealing. They'd dressed up and gone out to build a snowman. And to protect their new friend from the winter sun, they applied Nana's lotion on the snow pile so that he wouldn't tan. The result was a lumpy pile of oddly smelling snow.

But the family joined in on the fun. They got some burnt charcoal from the fireplace for its eyes and buttons, and Mom found an old carrot for its nose. Nana handed over twigs from one of the freezing trees, and everyone stood back to appraise the Forester snowman that would never melt or tan.

PRETENSE PERFORMANCE

Dave's four-year-old would tell you that love is getting to eat ice cream before dinner. But for Dave, it's different. Before meeting the love of his life, he was a self-conscious man.

His health ensured low stamina and slow metabolism for life. He'd hold his breath to pretend to people that he wasn't worn out by a single flight of stairs. When Dave ate out with friends, he'd eat less than half the food the others would have, just because they seemed to stay thin without any kind of worry or exercise. To have strangers deem him acceptable was exhausting.

Maria didn't care. His wife never hated when he was winded by a brisk walk or had several medications to take with his meals. She helped him cook the best foods that suited his metabolism and loved him when he was bone-tired from meager physical activity. Dave never pretended with her. She respected the beautiful and the ugly sides of him. He learned to take the good with the bad. Love had no pretense between them.

MIRROR FRIENDS

Smokey, the four-year-old cat, did not understand the tiny human Rob and Diana brought home from the hospital. He'd crawled under the couch anytime the baby was awake and squealing.

Rob worried that Smokey hated their daughter, and Diana wanted to calmly introduce the cat to her. But the cat wouldn't sit still enough to sniff the baby's bald head.

It was an odd few months conquered by the constant nighttime feeding and crying. Smokey stayed out of the baby's sight for a while.

One day, Diana had plopped her daughter in front of the closet mirror, and Smokey watched from afar. The baby was engrossed by her reflection. She slapped her palms on the mirror and squealed. Her eyes flickered, and she caught the cat's reflection.

Her smile dimmed, but it helped. The tiny front teeth poking through her gums were not visible, and Smokey advanced. The cat and baby stared at each other's reflections.

Perhaps the real friendship was discovering that both creatures had identical twins locked behind solid glass.

VEG TO VEGAN

Delilah announced that she was going vegan. Her friends were silent, wondering if this would cut down on their outings.

At first, it did. She'd eat dishes of tofu, fruit, and veggies only. Most eateries around the city didn't offer a huge variety of vegan food. Delilah wondered if her friends would ditch her and meet up elsewhere. It would hurt, but she was adamant.

Instead, her friends sneaked in pieces of fruit in their purses when they ate out. If the menus didn't have good options, Delilah knew she had the choice of fruit. Emboldened by their wholehearted acceptance, she, too, packed bland but intriguing snacks of tofu, syrup, and sauce.

It became a competition to sneak food into restaurants. Once in a while, they were caught and reprimanded. Delilah watched in awe when her friends retorted about the lack of food variety. Sometimes they were kicked out, and sometimes they had a stern warning. They'd never made fun of her for it. She was happy to be a vegan and proud to be their friend.

THE SECOND TOOTHBRUSH

Melissa was at her first sleepover at Stacy and Angie's house. And she'd forgotten her second toothbrush.

"What?" Angie laughed. "Why d'you need two?"

"It's for my hair."

Stacy and Angie stared. They'd never heard of anything like this. No one in the movies ever used toothbrushes on their hair!

"I guess Mom has an unopened one in the downstairs bathroom?" Stacy shrugged. Angie went to get it. Stacy sat and watched Melissa squirt hair moisturizing lotion onto her palm and massage it into her tight, coily hair. Then she touched up the tiny, short strands that formed the hairline around her temples and forehead.

Angie brought the new toothbrush, and Melissa accepted it with thanks. The girls observed her using the soft bristles to flatten the short curls onto the skin of her face, rotating the brush to form swirling circles of hair strands. She did this all around and stepped back from the mirror.

"Legally Blonde 2?" Melissa chirped, and the girls cuddled together to watch Elle Woods at it again (Herman-Wurmfeld, 2003).

FRUIT SANDWICH

Anything that sounded silly and quirky came within Dan's purview. This week, he challenged his sister, Rosie, to make a fruit sandwich.

Sunday morning was the perfect time to test it. They eagerly set up their stations in the kitchen to build a delicious fruit sandwich in the shortest amount of time. Or, at least, Dan was. Rosie just wandered about, totally relaxed.

"Half an hour, Rosie!" he snapped.

"I'll get it done in under ten seconds," she smirked.

If she thought she could just slice up different pieces of fruit and smush them between two bread slices that fast, she had another thing coming.

Dan arranged strawberries, mango, apple, banana, pumpkin, lettuce, and mayo. He layered his triangle-cut bread with alternating slices of the fruit based on color and taste. The lettuce would let him spread the mayo across the fruit.

Rosie dragged her feet to the island and whipped out mixed fruit jam. She slapped it on one side of a bread slice and dropped another slice on top of it. Done.

PHOTO SECRECY

Sierra was three when she saw an old photograph tucked into Abuelo's wallet. She immediately urged him to hand it over, and when he obliged, she observed the face of a pretty woman in it.

"Is this your girlfriend, Abuelo?"

Abuelo chuckled. "She used to be. Not anymore, though."

Sierra thought this over. "Did you break up with her like in the movies?"

"Not exactly. Time happened, and we've come a far way from where we started."

She didn't understand this. "Do you have a new girlfriend now, Abuelo?"

"I don't have any girlfriends now," he laughed. "But I married this woman. So, she's not my girlfriend anymore."

Sierra gawked at him. Then she stared at the photo closely before whispering, "Did you tell Abuela about her?"

NAME GAME

Charlie named her kids Sammy, Bradley, and Leslie. Ever since infancy, they were dressed in neutral clothes with contrasting colors. Neighborhood folks could never tell who were girls and who were boys. After living in that cul-de-sac for four months and having quick morning chats with her, the neighbors were reluctant to broach the subject.

The years passed. All three kids grew their hair, and Charlie braided them. But they'd also dress in T-shirts and shorts to play around in the mud. Were they boys with long hair and a hippie mom? Were they scruffy tomboyish girls and a liberal mom?

When Coco, Debbie's kid, celebrated her fourth birthday, she invited her friends for a bouncy house party. Sammy, Bradley, and Leslie arrived with matching grins. Charlie handed over a neatly wrapped gift and let her hoard loose in the backyard. All three kids hugged their mom before running outdoors.

Debbie smiled. What had been a mystery didn't seem to matter anymore. These kids were loved. They were happy and safe. What else mattered?

CAKE DECORATE

On Mason's 68th birthday, his grandkids pitched in and bought his favorite ice cream cake. The other grown-ups sat back and watched them decorate the house with gusto.

They surprised him with cake for lunch, and the crowded house burst with color and wonder all day. The party ended when the kids began tossing handfuls of cake at each other. They were stopped quickly, but Mason looked around and bellowed with laughter at the mess in the living room. The cake had splattered on the curtains, walls, floors, and people! They spent ages cleaning it out.

Some days later, the kids discovered cake on the ceiling. They'd missed that before. Cake splatter had solidified against the plaster.

They told no one.

Twenty years later, the splatter stains remained. The grown-ups had no clue. The kids giggled every time they saw it.

Mason was curious at the odd laughter and managed to bribe his adult grandkids with snacks. It worked. They pointed at the ceiling. The house was filled with the same roaring laughter that they loved.

PET CALL

Tina was pet-sitting her cousin's puppy, Seuss. He was a bundle of energy, and no number of toys satisfied him. He preferred to bite her couch and howl at night. Tina had never looked after a pet before.

On Monday, Seuss was restless and whiny. She had to cuddle him while she worked, or he'd start crying.

During a video call with her colleagues, Seuss began to jump on her lap. She was worried he'd disturb the call, but all her colleagues were delighted. Tina mentioned she was new to this and didn't know much about housing puppies.

Her friends showed off their pets. Tina met three cats, two dogs, and a snake! The people who didn't have companions were also eager. They shared good resources with her.

"Check the routine your cousin set!" one of them said. "Specific times for food, daily walks, and playtime. Be strict but gentle about alone time."

By the time the call was done, she was way more confident. Tina kissed Seuss on the head and knew they'd be alright.

LOVE AT FIRST CRASH

Levi's mother had been six when she'd finally learned to ride a bike without the training wheels. She was one of the first kids in the neighborhood to manage it and was very proud of it. A boy across the street didn't like it and wanted to catch up soon. He tried to wrench the side wheels off of his bike as well. Levi's mom caught him at it but decided to help the "little kid" in his mission.

They broke the bars that held the training wheels, and the boy was ecstatic, jumping on the seat and trying to cycle. He kept falling, so Levi's mom steadied the bike as he pedaled. She ran and pushed him ahead. For a few seconds, he pedaled happily on two wheels.

Then he lost control, fell, and scraped up his arms.

His mom rode with him for a full week until he could ride on his own. Levi's father loves telling this story. Even now, nearly fifty years after that crash, they're the best of friends.

SIBLING THINGS

When Chelsea remarried and had a daughter, her teen son from her first marriage wasn't happy. Max didn't connect with his new blended family.

Funny enough, Denise was curious about her older brother. She'd always crawl up to him and pull on his pants, eager to play with him. When she turned three, she managed to get into his room and rifle through his things.

Denise loved his skateboard. Chelsea had to rush her daughter out before he came back from school, lest he complained about it. But one day, Max caught his sister trying to ride his board.

To everybody's surprise, he helped her. Max steadied her on the board and let her ride it. She'd always laugh out loud when she played with him.

Chelsea watched as Max taught Denise how to ride a skateboard. He even took her to the local park to try it out with the big kids. He soon helped her with her bicycle and her schoolwork.

Denise is in high school now. She and Max are still close as ever.

HOME SUPPORT

Georgina moved in with her mother, Marisa, for a few months. As an IT technician, she was busy but inflexible. Marisa called her all the time.

"The computer's dead!"

"This captcha's wrong."

"What does this form want?"

The complaints stacked up constantly. Georgina gritted her teeth and helped out, but soon, the same problems kept cropping up.

"Is the power switch on?" Georgina snapped. "And read the text before you fill in any fields."

"I don't know all this tech stuff, like you."

Georgina would rather couch surf than stay here. But she gave it one last chance.

"Mom," she whispered, "When you moved out, did you ask others to help all the time, or did you learn chores?"

"It's not the same," Marisa retorted. "I never took a computer course!"

"It's the internet!" Georgina beseeched. "Google stuff! Check how to fill out forms and captchas. Use the same learning skills you do for everything else."

Later, there were no complaints, just quiet conversations. A hesitant truce settled over the house, and the pair managed it.

THE SAFE BET

Barny was left-handed, and the school art room didn't have safety scissors that he could use properly. He wanted to cut out the angel pieces he'd drawn so neatly. While the other kids carefully cut their pictures, he sat to the side, withdrawn.

The art teacher quickly called Mr. Tate from the faculty room and handed him some cash. Mr. Tate drove to four stationary stores around town before he found a colorful set of left-handed safety scissors for Barny and anyone else who needed them.

The kids were enthralled by the idea of having things everyone could use. They even cheered when Barny cut out his angel pieces. Mr. Tate later talked to the principal, and soon, the rooms with single chairs and attached desks also had chairs for left-handed folks. This helped all classes and some teachers as well. When Mr. Tate retired a few years later, Barny was the first to hug him. It had seemed like a small thing at first, but it made a world of difference for many people.

DARTS AND CARDS

Josh loved throwing darts with the boys. Despite the passing of decades, his gang always managed to find time to hang out for drinks and darts. It was a tradition to play a few rounds and chat about their families, friends, and jobs.

But when Donny had tremors in his hands, and Marley developed carpal tunnel, they played less in case the darts flew and hit unfortunate targets.

Josh was diagnosed with mild arthritis in his wrists soon. He hated the idea of things changing like this. If more of the guys had issues, they'd have to drop their games altogether. Sure, pool and foosball were always good options, but they'd been playing darts for a few decades.

Then, Billy suggested cards. Armed with regular playing cards, the gang gathered in front of a soft foam board to try out this new game. Josh grew to love it. Even though his wrists ached, and he knew he was quite past his prime, he still had a treasure trove of people surrounding him.

GRAY HAIRS

Meg was 15 when she found her first gray hair. Her horrified mother helped pluck the strand.

At first, she went with it. Who wanted gray hairs in sophomore year? But soon, Meg found more pale strands in her rich brown hair. When her grandma discovered this, she shared all-natural shampoos and hair mask recipes with Meg.

After a few years of plucking and dyeing it brown, Meg was done. She went to the parlor and came back with bright pink hair.

"There," Meg said with a newfound boldness. "No gray hairs."

"You're still in school, Margaret!" her mom groaned.

"I'm an adult," Meg reminded her. "This is my hair. I'll cut it, style it, and dye it my way, Mom. No tweezers or horrible-smelling shampoos and conditioners."

"So you went with bleach," her mother asked faintly.

"Yes. Hair is supposed to grow gray. Just because it started early doesn't mean I need to bend over backward to stop it. I was fine with gray. I'm happy with pink. And I'll be good with gray again."

THE GO-TO GIFT

Megan was terrible at gift-giving. She wasn't the best at recalling what her friends and family would say they needed during the year. When her sister's birthday loomed over the horizon, Megan was at a loss.

Impersonal items like coffee mugs never fit the theme. Becky wasn't a grand tea or coffee drinker.

Finally, she decided to write a birthday card.

"Dear Becks,

Here's to another year with you. I didn't know what to get you, so I hope you won't be too mad. But I wanted to say that you're doing amazing things, and it's incredible to see someone go out and just reach for the things they want. You've always been bold with your life and wonderful to all of us. I'm proud to call you a sister and a friend. Let's find ways to hang out more; maybe I'll know what to get you for your next birthday!

Love, Megan."

Becky loved it!

"We should definitely hang out!" she cried. "You're the best, Megan. You always know just what to say!"

STAR STORIES

Patrick's youngest granddaughter accidentally let go of her helium balloon. It soared instantly, escaping into the stratosphere.

Three-year-old Sania wailed and pointed at her lost toy growing smaller in the sky. Patrick picked her up and hugged her tight. "It's alright, Sania. I'll get you another balloon."

"No!" she shrieked, her face turning red.

"But your balloon went on an adventure, baby," Patrick blurted. "He had to go visit the moon, see?"

He showed her the pale moon just visible in the daytime. Sania's sobbing slowed.

"That's where your balloon went," Patrick said in relief. "He loves the sky, so he's going to fly high up and find all the stars."

She glared at him. "No buh-bye?"

Patrick nodded and kissed her cheek. "He was so excited to go that he forgot to say goodbye. But that means he'll come back and tell you all his moon and star stories. Would you like that?"

She nodded with a smile. In a week, Patrick would have to get her another helium balloon and hope for the best.

CABLE COMPLIANCE

When Victoria wanted some alone time, she'd assign sneaky little chores to her grandkids to keep them busy. She'd dropped coins in the storeroom, and the kids eagerly shifted papers and books out of the way to find them. It helped give more legroom in the utility space. Once she gave them a magnifying glass and asked them to find a butterfly in the garden, which they did happily.

This time she held up an old DVD.

"It's a comedy from the 1950s," Victoria told the little ones. "It's got jokes, songs, and dances. But I need to find the right cable for the DVD player."

"I'll find it!"

"No, me!"

The voices erupted, and the kids leaped behind the TV to find a knotted set of cables covered in dust. Victoria unplugged the spike buster to avoid accidents and set them to it.

An hour later, all the cables were rearranged, and the kids were watching Singin' in the Rain with her. It was the only way she could get them to watch old-timey pictures.

YARN LOVE

Sara's comfort labor was knitting. She found the repetitive motions soothing. This time, she was working on sweaters.

She'd planned to go by order. Two great-grandchildren, five grandkids, three children plus their three spouses, and one wife. Fourteen handmade sweaters coming right up!

Having never made sweaters before, it would probably take her most of the year to get them ready. She wasn't a pro at this, but it made her mind run on the various kinds of designs she wished she could incorporate especially relevant things.

A cuckoo bird would fit little Joey regarding that time when the baby had done nothing all day except wait for the cuckoo clock to chirp on the hour. A leaf pattern was perfect for Janice, who had admitted her secret desire to dive into a pile of dry leaves in the fall. Sara could think of several incidents that covered the rag-tag bunch that made up her joyous family.

Maybe that could be a project for next year. Right now, she stayed in the moment and continued her knitting.

SAND RACER

Some of Julie's friends have trendy childhood memories of racing with their dads and grandmas that inspired them to join the track teams. She wanted that, so her grandfather suggested she practice running on the beach.

Julie didn't know what was so different about running there versus running on tar. But the moment she stepped on the loose sand, she knew.

"I can't run on the sand!" she complained.

Her grandfather just shrugged, "Try it."

So she did. The sand dragged her feet down no matter much she managed to pick up the pace. It was hard, and she simply couldn't gain any traction.

Ten minutes after failing to run on the beach, she turned back and said, "It's not happening! No one can run on sand."

Her grandfather laughed. "You can if you practice it every day. It's hard to run through water or on the sand. But that's how some great racers practice. If you can find an edge here, you'll zip right through your races and also have a cool backstory!"

PAINT PRINTS

Leona's parakeet was a few months old and routinely disturbed her as she painted. She spent long hours painting only to find that Eddie would fly by to inspect the smell and the flash of color. Then he'd walk over the wet paint before she could shoo him off.

"Eddie, stop it!" she'd complain, but he flew up to the dresser and observed her anyway.

She'd take another hour fixing the ruined paint, and he'd watch the whole time. Leona loved the bird; she really did. Still, he was way too young to understand the importance of her paintings.

But one day, he understood.

Leona looked up from her work to find Eddie perched very close to the painting. She cringed, but he did not step on the wet canvas. Instead, he ducked his head and observed the underside of his claws before stepping around the painting. Every time he checked his claws, Leona's heart swelled.

Animals suited her because she was asocial with people but gentle with the former. They were gentle with her as well.

FOSTER POWER

When Charlie fostered her first kitten, she had it all planned. Three-day-old Toby would be fed once every two hours. Charlie had to wake up at night to bottle-feed the baby. The kitten was too young to play. He ate and slept on repeat.

She watched him open his watery eyes and unfold his tiny ears. Within a week, he was trying to stand up instead of just wriggling about. Soon, Charlie was tossing little cat toys at Toby and reveled in the way he'd pounce on the fluffy toys, his little claws outstretched.

She bathed him, got him his vaccines, and had him micro-chipped before potential adopters called in. Eight-week-old Toby meowed and blinked at her on his last day. Charlie wept when his new parents left with him, completely thrilled by the kitten. She wished she could have kept him. But fostering is a powerful act, and Charlie knew she could help take care of more kittens and make sure they are loved and cherished in any appreciative household. That's what foster parents do.

CHAPTER 3

JOURNEY AND ADVENTURES

LINGUA FRANCA

Delia's family was polylingual. They were scattered around Canada but kept in touch as much as possible. As a result, Delia grew up hearing French, Italian, Spanish, Portuguese, bits of Greek, and English.

People often mentioned how incredible it was to witness the family talk between themselves. Once, the family as a whole went on a small nature hike. Their jovial guide was impressed by their conversations. He'd never known a group of people to speak so easily in different tongues. Delia's grandpa would ask a question in French, and her Mom would answer in Italian, while her brothers would pitch in with sparse knowledge of Spanish.

Apparently, they were the most fun group the tour guide had taken in years. He brought them through some of the more adventurous routes, which had the family crossing a tiny stream, trekking through the denser areas, and even reaching a high cliff that looked over the Atlantic.

It was always a wonder when Delia's people impressed others just by being themselves.

MUGGY DAYS

When Dennis retired, he began a coffee mug collection. His kids and grandkids loved the idea and gifted him several interesting mugs with designs that ranged from awe-inspiring to plain silly. Some of his favorites were the ones with quirky inscriptions.

- "Superman without his coffee is just Barely-Awake-Man."
- "A coin is three-dimensional, yet we only consider its two faces."
- "James Bond's watch has his flair. It goes tock, tick tock."
- "Love helps us grow greater than our pain."

The best mugs were in his silver collection case. Dennis and his wife traveled widely and managed to buy mugs from small stalls in towns across Europe and Asia. Over the years, he'd amassed beautiful mugs, some of which were hand carved, shaped like birds and animals, in a wild variety of colors, and even of the kintsugi style.

When people gawked at his incredible and eclectic collection, Dennis preened, glad to be able to travel and bring back such jolly souvenirs.

STAR-STUDDED DREAMS

Robbie and a few fellow teachers chaperoned a school trip where they brought groups of students out near the desert campout. When he performed a headcount, he found one extra kid.

Second-grader May had wandered from one of the other groups and ended up at his camp.

"I'm going to call Miss Sanchez to pick you up," Robbie told her sternly.

May nodded, barely aware of what he had told her. She was gazing at the sky filled with millions of stars and cosmic gas clouds.

Robbie grinned. "First time outside the city, May?"

She nodded.

"Yeah, we don't really see stars like this back home."

"Why not?"

"Light and gas pollution. Streetlights, building beacons, neon lights, and clouds of gas add up. They blur out the fainter stars. But out here, we see so much more."

May nodded, utterly entranced. Robbie enjoyed watching students fall in love with what teachers introduced to them. He hoped May would go on to follow her dreams with as much passion as she stared at the sky.

CAMELIA'S TEETH: II

Camelia was on her way for the first session of a root canal treatment. She found the roads blocked due to a misaligned traffic signal and had to divert.

She zoomed across town using her GPS to find a way through the crossroads, the one-way streets, and the crowded sections to reach her destination.

Being geographically illiterate was her downfall. The second time she hit a dead end, Camelia began to panic. She couldn't afford to postpone the root canal. She missed eating ice cream, and everything too cold or too hot ached her teeth and gums. She needed to reach the appointment on time!

Plan B: Ask for directions.

Camelia stopped by a grocer and enquired about a landmark near her dentist. The grocer gave good directions, and she was off, zipping down the roads to reach the right street.

She was glad not to be frightened of drills and saws. Otherwise, she might have skipped the appointment altogether!

SMILE IN SOLITUDE

Priya was the last single cousin standing in the extended family and still managed to weather the loud and snarky comments of "spinster" and "commitment-phobic" she received every month.

But the yearly family trip was coming up. It was four days' worth of snide remarks disguised in sweet voices.

"Maybe you'll meet a cute skiing instructor," her mother whispered as they left their hotel rooms.

"Maybe you'll let me live my life," Priya shot back.

"You're 32, Priya. You're going to get lonely soon."

Sigh. All her cousins were married, some with kids. Priya greeted them distantly and headed up the mountain with her skis. She caught a seat up and relaxed in the brisk air.

Her ears pricked with the rush of blood. No sound reached her. Priya loved the solitude of her thoughts. She'd have to face her family again when she skied down the hill, but for now, she didn't have to have any walls up. Priya constantly found moments of peace on her own, a true power of the singles.

WHALE OF A TIME

Dana ran a small nonprofit group near the coast that cleaned up beaches with volunteers.

Three years into the job, he and the team found a beached whale. He went on a call with a consultant from National Oceanic and Atmospheric Administration and understood that the poor wriggling whale needed to be "refloated" before they could release it.

The NOAA team donned protective gloves and suits. A bulldozer was hired to dig sand away from the flapping tail. They tied a heavy leather belt around the whale to get the machine to pull it toward the ocean.

Dana's group kept bystanders away from the scene and brought buckets of water to keep the whale's skin wet. They also splashed water on the sand around its body.

Luck was on the whale's side; the entire team put their backs into it and managed to get the lower half into the receding waterline. The whale flapped into an oncoming tide, and responders snipped the belt, freeing the whale. They cheered as the whale disappeared under the water.

QUEST THROUGH TOWN

When Sandy lost Caleb's old stuffed panda toy, she knew he would not take this loss well. Aunt Bailey wrote a list of places Sandy had been in town—the local mart, park, diner, and library.

They trekked through the mart, walking by several aisles to conclude that it wasn't there. The pair left for the park to check around the sand pit and jungle gyms in vain.

The diner yielded no such lost toys as well. Bailey drove them down to the library, hopeful. But even with the librarian's help, they found no panda.

Finally, her aunt, Bailey, mom, and dad helped her build the courage to tell her friend that she'd lost his best toy. Caleb, predictably, wailed and ran home. But Aunt Bailey promised Sandy that she'd done the right thing. She'd retraced her steps to search everywhere and then admitted the truth.

"Maybe we can get Caleb a book on pandas?" she suggested to Sandy. "He's hurting now, but don't worry. You're a good friend."

THE SOLO TRIP

When her daughter had her third child, Josie flew over to help out. It was nerve-wracking because she'd never traveled so far alone before. Her husband or sisters usually accompanied her but not this time. Josie was 67, ready to fly all by herself.

Check-in, boarding pass, and security—that was the process. With her case on the conveyor belt, the staff checked her ticket and asked, "Where are you going?"

"Salt Lake City," Josie mumbled.

"What is the purpose of your visit?"

"To see my daughter. Um, not on business."

The staff worker grinned. "Have a good trip, Ma'am!"

Josie practically snatched the pass and hurried toward security. She placed all her belongings on the tray, held her pass tight, and went through the metal detector. It didn't beep, and she sighed in relief.

The flight was decent, and when they landed in Utah, Josie was joyous. She'd done it! She'd always been scared to travel, but with some good preparation, she'd managed it. Josie couldn't wait to travel solo again.

CRACKER PLANTS

Missy was down in the dumps, so her aunt, April, and grandma, Phyllis, took her out to a rough meadow. It was a small trek to the spot. Though Missy wasn't in the mood for a picnic, she knew her grandma was very keen on finding the loveliest plants.

Aunt April found what they were searching for. Missy gasped at the beautiful purple flowers around them. But Grandma showed her the real attraction. "These are cracker plants, sweetie. Their seeds burst out when they fall in the water."

She, Missy, and her aunt pluck the small, long, and hard seeds, dropping them in an empty cup. Missy poured water and waited.

It took just a couple of seconds for the explosions to start. She jumped back and laughed as the seeds burst open, sending tiny beady fillings everywhere! Each seed popped once, and she grinned as things slowed down.

"Again!" Missy cried and ran off to find more seeds. She couldn't wait to tell all her friends!

CAMELIA'S TEETH: III

When Camelia had to have a wisdom tooth removed, she opted for local anesthesia. No laughing gas for her. It was on the lower jaw, and Camelia was alone at the dentist's because her family couldn't handle the drill.

Her husband was terrified of dentists, and neither of her daughters would even willingly go to a clinic unless they had problems. Dental treatment was Camelia's alone time, so to speak. She'd been cycling herself to clinics for years.

She got a double shot of anesthesia and waited until the entire side of the jaw right up to her eye went numb. The extra dose was to ensure nothing would pinch because, apparently, her bone structure was one of the densest types the dentists had come across. The last time he operated on her teeth, he needed another doctor's helping hands to reach into the lower jawbone to remove the tooth. Did you know the lower wisdom teeth were directly connected to the jawbone? Camelia's were. Her teeth were a marvel in the medical world.

THE MOVIE GANG

Cecilia had been going to the movies every month with her sisters for most of their adult lives. If you can imagine four women in their 70s giggling as they buy tickets for rom-com and Hallmark films, you've nailed them.

A while ago, the schedule lined up without many light-hearted options.

"Maybe we can stay home and binge Fleabag?" Ronnie suggested.

"Oh, we'd never finish it before midnight," Cecelia replied.

Isadora pointed at one of the posters, "How about The Expendables?"

Everyone stared at her.

Maxine burst into snort-filled laughter, "Izzy! That's not really our type."

"No. But Cece's right; I don't want to go home and binge anything."

"But that's such a guy movie?"

"It's a nonperfect, bad story that people watch for fun," Isadora said, "Don't knock it till you try it, ladies."

The others finally conceded. It was ever a sight to see four large women with graying perms get tickets for The

Expendables. Bad stories come in all forms, but with the right attitude and gang, you'll get a good experience.

SKYDIVING

Irene was 100 when she went skydiving for the first time. Tandem jumps were routine for amateurs, but the diving team was startled by the old lady who applied for the diving run.

She surprised everyone by passing the health check-up and interview. Irene was fearless to the extent she inspired others to try it out. She was hooked up to her partner on the plane before they leaped out more than 10,000 feet above sea level!

With the cold wind rushing by, Irene had never felt so alive! Her partner, Jed, was just as thrilled as her as they tried different poses in the sky until they were simply free-falling. When Jed gave her the signal that he was about the open the parachute, Irene held on to her buckles, grinning wide.

The parachute burst open and nearly yanked them to a halt in mid-air. They could easily see the drop zone now, with several people milling about like ants. When they landed, everyone jumped about, congratulating Irene for her daredevilry.

GOLDEN SAND

Mike was observing the shimmering sand around his house when the three youngest members of the family spilled out.

"Baba! What're you doing?" one of them cheered.

Mike grinned. "I'm looking for gold."

The kids paused. "Huh?"

"See how the sand shines?" Mile swiped some gravel into his hand and poured it back out. "That's gold."

"Whoa! We're rich!" his granddaughter cried.

"We're well-off," Mike conceded. "My grandfather was a goldsmith. He used to sit there on the porch and fix jewelry all day long. He sat there for years working so much that gold dust settled in the sand."

The kids gasped and shouted things together.

"So much gold!"

"You had a Baba?"

"You're old, Baba!"

Mike grasped the youngest and swung her up. She laughed wildly.

"My Baba made all kinds of pretty things for people," he told them. "Our family doesn't do this anymore, but the gold is still here."

"Can we get it out, Baba?" the oldest asked.

"Yes," he murmured before winking. "But I like the way the sand shines."

WAITING

Sandy and Imran spent four years pursuing adoption agencies for their one and only wish: to have a child. They were middle-aged, and this deterred a lot of firms. But one rainy day, they were called for an interview.

It had the standard queries: reasons for adopting, medical health, and career plans. Finally, the agent said, "We may have an opening for you."

It wasn't promising, so Sandy and Imran didn't get their hopes up. But when they got the call, they dropped everything and rushed to the car.

An infant wrapped in an old comforter with no mention of birth parents waited for them. Imran accepted the sniffling child, and Sandy signed the required documents.

Despite fears of being too old for kids, Sandy and Imran had no reason to change their minds. This was a new adventure for them, waiting to teach them things they'd always wanted to learn.

SALTY AND SWEATY

Olivia bought a salt lamp as a birthday gift for her great-aunt Hanna. Despite the pouring rain, she still cycled down the street and picked it up. Carefully protecting it with bubble wrap, she biked back to the house and brought it inside. None of the rain touched the lamp, but to be safe, Olivia wiped it down with a dry cloth.

Unfortunately, the next day, she and Hanna found it in a puddle of colored water on the table. It even dripped down onto the floor, filling the room with an odd and stale smell.

“It’s leaking!” Olivia said, aghast. “But it never even got wet!”

Hanna squinted at the lamp. “It’s the humidity, my dear. Let’s just dry everything off. It’s bound to rain for the rest of the week.”

“So, it’s going to cry for the whole week?”

“We call it sweating.”

Olivia laughed. “Salt lamps are better than what I imagined. They can run, they can sweat; next thing you know, they’ll be competing in marathons!”

HEARING HELP

Samuel's hearing aid stopped working when he was at the grocery store. The high-pitched ringing that usually persisted suddenly kicked up a notch, deafening everything else.

He winced and cupped his hands over his ears, searching for help. Samuel reached the checkout, and the cashier saw him. She quickly approached him and made the motion to place her palms over his ears.

The noise was really bothering him, so he was ready for anything. The girl placed the base of her palms over his gnarled fingers, pressing down firmly. Her fingers came over the base of his skull, and with deliberate motion, she snapped her fingers over the skin.

Once, twice, thrice…

The noise dulled. Samuel blinked, stunned. He dislodged his hands and looked at her wide-eyed. The cashier grinned and said in a now audible voice, "Tinnitus, huh? Yeah. That gets really bothersome. You're good?"

Samuel nodded. Aside from her, everything else was absolutely quiet. His ears always had some sort of noise for years.

The silence was a gift not many appreciated. Samuel would appreciate this.

ECCENTRIC TASTE

Edith was in charge of catering a school dance. She ran a bakery and assigned a team to cook and bake the menu requirements. But when she ducked into the bakery to check on her staff, she was met with disaster. The little palm-sized cakes and muffins were misshapen.

Apparently, one of the youngsters had not stirred the batter well enough and had baked the lumpy batter for all the pastries. The taste was fine, but Edith would never allow her bakery to sell such terribly made muffins.

They restarted with a fresh batch, and Edith considered the bad pastries. Throwing them out ached her. Batter smoothness was an unsaid policy for these pastries. But October was ending. Could she…?

Edith placed the pastries behind the curved glass wall as free samples. One would never know if they didn't try.

Testing them as pre-Halloween treats were great! People actually took the cakes. Maybe they thought the idea was eccentric or silly, but they still ate them, and Edith began planning customized Halloween treats.

THE GARDEN MAZE

Janice and Beverly visited a small hedge maze in Luray where they'd successfully gotten lost! The maze was smaller than the parking lot, but it still offered them lots of fun. With garden walls towering at eight feet, they couldn't cheat in any way.

Beverly's strategy was to place her left hand on the garden wall and simply walk until they reached the exit. Janice followed, but she was also on the lookout for maps.

"Why would they leave us maps?" Beverly asked, incredulous.

"Because we're guests, not participants in the Hunger Games," Janice laughed. "They wouldn't really want us to get lost!"

Half an hour of walking actually led them to a wooden signpost built beside one of the hedge walls. Janice eagerly took its photo, and they continued on a new path. They passed by other people also exploring the maze, wandering past many forks and dead ends before finally exiting the maze!

"The map did help," Beverly conceded. "Ready for lunch?"

"Yes! And then another trip into the maze."

"Of course!"

SWIMMING SOCIALITES

The public pool was reserved for seniors on Tuesdays and Saturdays. Irvin and Maureen were at the pool for the first time, hopeful to meet others in the neighborhood.

They chatted with George, a bachelor living just two blocks from their apartment. He'd been swimming since he was in his 50s and made most social connections right at the pool.

Barry and Nancy were visiting their son in the States. They chatted about air travel and how small airplane seats are nowadays.

Ginger and Alex were another couple at the pool who'd been coming on and off for more than 10 years. They knew all kinds of swimming techniques.

Bill was the youngest of them at 64. He had hydrotherapy lessons with a guide in the pool to alleviate the pain in his back. Irvin left him to it and swam around in a loop to reach Maureen, out of breath.

"We needed this experience! We'll come back on Saturday," she said happily.

"Or let's just stick to once a month," Irvin gasped, already out of breath.

NIGHT LIGHTS

Wallace and Eve made their way to King Eider Inn in Northern Alaska. He checked them into a room with large windows facing north.

Ever since Eve was little, she'd always wanted to see the northern lights. The idea of waves of lights bursting into colors along the sky had been too fantastical. But several books, movies, and blogs boasted about the aurora borealis. It became part of her bucket list.

She and Wallace lived in Juneau for most of their lives. A few friends traveled to Canada to witness the lights, but northern parts of Alaska received an equal dose of delight.

They were right. Wallace and Eve cuddled up on the bed under the comforter; hands cupped around mugs of hot coffee. The shutters to their windows were wide open, and the northern lights danced across the dark sky, lighting up everything around them. The lights flickered like curtains in the wind, and Eve caught pink, green, blue, and even yellow ribbons against the sky's dark backdrop! The drive-up had been worth it.

CHAPTER 4

HUMOR AND LAUGHTER

PAPER PROGRESS

My great-aunt was a lecturer at the community college nearby. She came across some creative and brilliant minds every year, but her favorite thing to do was find absentminded or oddly-phrased answers in the students' assignments.

- The pen is mightier than the sword, but the sword is pointier. That's why Attila the Hun conquered so many places.
- Laissez-Faire was a fair economy for the French in the 19th century.
- The Cold War began when the US realized they could not fight Russia in the winter like Napoleon Bonaparte.
- The government planted a lot of vines to help solve the 1930s Great Depression.
- People in the 1980s didn't have many ways to save music other than scratched records and flopped disks.

- The oldest trees have the greatest number of rings in their bark. But it's proven that cutting them down to confirm the rings is unhelpful.
- The Leaning Tower of Pisa stands tall in Italy. It's called Torre Pendente di Pizza in Italian.

HEIR'S HAIR CONCERNS

Allen's youngest granddaughter couldn't understand why he never had the latest hair trends. She tried showing him pictures online of K-Pop stars with flouncy hair and wondered if he'd ever go for that.

"I'm afraid I can't, sweetie," Allen would tell her. "I'm past those styles."

"No, you're not!" she argued and pointed to a 30-year-old picture of him on the wall. "See? You used to have it like that! Just tell the nice barber to cut it like that!"

"I did have that once upon a time," Allen agreed. "But unless I suddenly stop being bald, it just ain't gonna happen!"

REAL PLASTIC

Sandra found a 10-year-old setting up a quaint lemonade stall. She hadn't seen one in years, so she hopped over to the kid and asked for a glass. The boy gleefully poured the large jug of lemonade into a paper cup and said, "That'll be $5!"

Five? Sandra nodded slowly and decided not to say anything. She handed over the cash and drank up the entire cup in seconds. It was wonderful!

"Wait a sec," the boy scowled. "Why is this plastic?"

"That's how they come," Sandra said, wondering if it would be too much to get another cup.

"Then why's it called paper money?" the kid pestered.

"It used to be made of paper," she replied. "But now it's plastic."

"Why?"

"Progress."

The boy grimaced. Sandra carefully asked, "I'd like another cup, please."

"Sure," he sighed before his eyes flashed. "Real paper money this time!"

BANK ON DAD

Sammy's Dad had retired a lifetime ago and was spry enough to take a trip uptown.

"I'm off to the bank!" he shouted to Sammy before lumbering out of the house. When he reached the place, the first teller took a look at his passbook and sent him across the road, saying, "Ah, sir. You've got the wrong bank."

Dad squinted at the sign that read, "UBS."

Wasn't that the United Bank of the States? To make sure that the young teller wasn't some upstart who was out to make his life harder, he rang up Sammy.

"Dad? Is everything alright?"

"What's my bank?!" his dad demanded.

"Bank of America," Sammy reminded him. "Opposite the deli store."

"They moved it!"

"They what now?"

"The deli is next to UBS!" Dad complained. "This woman won't let me in!"

"Dad, you're standing in front of the United Bank of Switzerland. Bank of America is across the street!"

The 21st century was incomprehensible. America and Switzerland are divided by a road and not an ocean and a continent? Outrageous!

NUMBER STUMBLE

Tara's parents lived in the penthouse of her apartment building while she was on the first floor. They almost always remembered her house number…except for the time that they didn't.

Her Dad hit the floor number, and they went down to 204. The door was open, and despite the distinct difference in the furniture, tiles, TV set, wallpaper, and the giant painting of a mermaid, they sat on the loveseat for five minutes before 204's occupant emerged from the bathroom after having bathed her dog.

It was a rather confusing moment, with the dog bouncing around them, still spraying droplets everywhere.

SALTY SLEEPER

Chastity was a night owl. She was late to bed and late to rise. This made getting ready for school an obstacle course for the entire household.

One family member was appointed to set a surprise alarm that would follow her usual alarm rings. Another member would bang on her door and run away. A third person would bring breakfast to her room to waft the smell into her face. They'd thought about using smelling salts but felt it extreme.

Most tricks only succeeded in annoying her. An irritated Chastity at a rushed breakfast never resulted in a good day. Most weeks went like this. Finally, her dad had had enough. He filled a bucket of water, marched into her room, and poured it over her.

She woke up with a shriek! "Dad! It's Sunday!"

"Sun's already high up," her father cried.

"Am I supposed to photosynthesize?!"

"Chas, next time, it will be the salts!"

Strangely enough, the threat worked, which was good because the family did not have smelling salts.

CONTACT LOST

Amelia's family was comprised of people with both shortsighted and longsighted vision. Nearly everyone wore glasses, and family get-togethers were a hazard on account of misplacing spectacles all over the place.

They'd accidentally exchange them or end up with someone else's glasses. The go-to prank in the household would be to mix up everyone's spectacles so the family would spend a blundering ten minutes just griping and moaning about it.

Amelia was eighteen when she opted for contact lenses. Surely, without the need for cumbersome glasses, she'd no longer have any problems with the change.

And yet, and yet…

Amelia always kept her lenses in their little case on her nightstand before going to bed. One night, she misplaced them and had to employ the entire family to help her search for a tiny blue case of lenses. It proved even more inconvenient than looking for glasses due to the size. They gave up after a few days, and Amelia returned to her spectacles. At least they were big enough for her to find them!

CHANGE FOR NONE

Cherian ordered a regular latte which cost $12.20. He handed over $15 and 20¢. The barista, Martin, frowned and replied, "Sir, you don't need to pay 20¢ extra."

And Cherian watched as Martin rifled for 80¢ to hand over to him along with $3.

"The remainder is actually $2 and 80¢," Cherian pointed out. "Or you could just take my 20¢ and give me $3."

Martin stared. "Sir, why would I do that?"

"'Cause $15.20 minus $12.20 is $3."

"What about the change?"

"It's right here!"

"But the price is $12.20, not $15, sir."

"Yes… but if I add the change, then you don't need to."

Martin blurted, "Sir, if you wish, you can place it in the tip jar."

"But—"

The manager dashed out, her hair in disarray. "Hello, sir! I'll take care of this for you. Martin, check on the backlog."

Cherian walked out aptly baffled. Martin learned nothing new that day.

SKY'S THE LIMIT

Tamara's parents were on the highway going fast enough to be pulled over by the cops. Her Mom was distressed because they were in a hurry and did not have time for any stops. But the officer was already writing the ticket.

"It's an emergency! We have to reach our daughter now. We can't wait!"

The officer nodded. "I understand, but I have to ticket anyone over 65."

Her Mom blurted, "That's discrimination!"

The officer paused and replied, "Ma'am, I mean the speed limit."

OPPOSITE DAY

Sammy's granddad commanded respect without raising his voice. And when he did yell, nobody dared cross him. When Sammy sneaked into the house past curfew, Granddad caught him. "Where were you?! Why are you so late?"

The teen whispered, "My friends and I were at the local diner. We just lost track of time."

"You should've called! Or you could have planned better! It's past midnight! Don't tell me you went to Pat-a-Cake's!"

Sammy gulped. He had been there. The late-night rush at Pat-a-Cake diner ensured every patron left late all the time.

"Umm," Sammy summoned some courage. "I didn't go to Pat-a-Cake. I also didn't fight over the bill and pay for Maddy because it's not her birthday. I didn't drive everyone home because it rained, and I didn't get stuck anywhere because the roads were totally not flooded!"

Granddad blinked before cackling out loud. Nobody had talked back to him in years. His grandson's retort was a breath of fresh air.

WINDOW ALERT

Coach Schmidt was due to retire soon, which was why the number of silly incidents among students rose exponentially in his last year. Just the other day, he'd left the kids on their own to attend an urgent phone call. When he returned, a window—the only glass thing in the gym room—was broken, and half the kids were missing.

"What happened this time?" he sighed.

The students burst out into rapid answers, and he only heard a few.

"Mary kicked the basketball, and it broke the window!"

"It also broke my toe!"

"Vanessa ran out the moment the glass broke, and the other girls ran after her."

"She didn't even do anything; I don't know why she left!"

"I have to go to the nurse, Coach Schmidt!"

The coach nodded. Well, no one ever said being a teacher was dull. He was going to miss the energy his students brought to the court every day. But retirement sounded wonderful.

Right after he explained to the principal why the window was broken.

THE RIGHT ANSWER

The microwave dinged, letting Mom know dinner was ready. She told her four-year-old daughter to get her dad. Little Kimmy eagerly climbed the stairs to summon her father with a terrific bellow.

After a few moments, she came back down, "Daddy'll eat later!"

Mom made a face. "He'll have to reheat it. Why's he late?"

"Because he's sleeping," Kimmy said dutifully.

"Can you wake him up?"

"Daddy said I can't jump on him anymore."

"Okay, just nudge him. We can have dinner as a family."

Kimmy nodded and went back up to the bedroom. Mom had arranged the table when the child came back to her and announced, "Daddy is sleeping super deep and can have food only later."

Mom sighed, "Fine! But why didn't the nudging work?"

Kimmy shrugged, "I poked him in the eye, but Daddy told me that he was sleeping so much he couldn't feel anything!"

NO MORE DOOR

Mr. Hubert of AP History was a pretty alright teacher, and the students rather liked him.

On sunny days, he'd propped open the door and latched the door stoppers. These were not the regular or springy ones at the bottom. Two palm-sized blocks of wood were built into the side hinges. With the door open, he could just flip the wooden blocks to stop the hinges from turning.

It was World Teacher's Day. We waited in class with confetti poppers to surprise him. The moment he walked in, we burst into greetings, noise, and a lot of cheery commotion. Mr. Hubert jumped and tried to shush us, laughing. But we were riding in high spirits and just kept yelling louder, so he dropped his bag and tried to slam the door to keep the noise in.

As you can guess, the door stoppers banged into the hinges and broke. The entire door fell out of the frame and crashed onto the floor.

So, that's why room 204 did not have a door until Christmas.

HUM, SOME MORE

Benny and Mary-Ann babysat their first grandkid, Izzy, to give her parents a break for the night. Izzy was nearly a year old and was a fairly easygoing toddler. She sat still enough when they watched a game on TV.

Just as it kicked off, Izzy muttered something. She moved her lips, strange sounds coming out. Her grandma leaned in to listen to the odd rambling.

“Is she scared?” Benny asked, sitting up. Mary-Ann was worried. This couldn’t be normal behavior, could it? None of her children ever made noises like that. To be safe, she rang up her daughter.

“Yeah, Mom?”

“Hi, Hun,” Mary-Ann said. “Don’t worry, Izzy’s fine. But she’s constantly mumbling something; we’re not sure what.”

Her daughter asked slowly, “Is the TV on?”

“Yes, we’re watching the game.”

They heard laughter over the phone. “Mom! That’s okay! Izzy’s singing the national anthem!”

Benny choked and leaned down to listen to his granddaughter. Sure enough, the tune of the Star-Spangled Banner was clearer now.

GREEN ROOM

When Will's daughter married and moved into a new house, she wanted a green room.

Will wanted to help. Paints, curtains, and tiles, along with wallpaper, cushions, and even lights, would be green!

What shade, though? Jenny was a small-time actress and would often bring her own make-up to shooting sets. She'd once said that forest-green nail polish was her favorite.

To be safe, Will called her up and dived head-first. "...so that's why I was wondering what tone you'd like for your green room."

Jenny paused. "Dad? That's not what I meant."

Will felt self-conscious. "Did you want another color?"

"No! OMG, I love you, Dad! A green room is just a separate place for me to dress up and get ready. Like a powder room. I was thinking I'd have a walk-in closet."

"Right," Will murmured.

"No, Dad, that's fantastic," Jenny grinned. "We can make the walk-in closet green! Wallpaper, paint, and tiles!"

Will smiled. He'd known the dad joke would win her over.

SHOCKING POWER

When Jasper was seven, he'd jammed a plastic fork into an electric socket. Even so, he felt a teeth-clattering crackle of energy through from his fingers up his arm and down his spine. It lasted less than a second before the fork broke.

The memory remained etched in his mind, but he had yearly reminders of the event. When winter rolled out, and the air was dry and cool, Jasper could elicit static energy with any metallic and woolen surface. Comforters, sweaters, taps, doorknobs, window grills, TVs, windchimes, et cetera.

It was his superpower. For years, when anyone annoying made it into his space, Jasper would rub his feet on the floor, fluff up his hair, and jab his finger into their arm. Instant spazz!

PAINT WITH POLISH

Desiree crashed her cycle into Nana's old Lexus and left scratch lines in the dark paint. It wasn't the end of the world, but Nana loved her car and made sure to keep it well-cleaned and serviced. Dents and marks were a no-no.

She planned to fix it herself. The blue paint mimicked the inkiness of the night sky, and Desiree knew that her mom had nail polish in the same shade. She stole into her parent's room and found the bottle in question.

She painted over the scratches with nail polish. Finishing the streaks with a flourish, Desiree could barely tell the difference! The car looked brand new!

However, a week later, Nana phoned the house, asking about strange grey lines of wobbly paint on her beloved car. Turns out the nail polish faded rather quickly and changed colors, now leaving ugly and very visible marks on the side of the car.

"Maybe, next time, you can just tell me when you want to fix something," Nana laughed.

HAUNTED LABS

The third-grade kids loved sneaking into the biology lab in the nearby high school building. It wasn't just the "big-kid" environment that invigorated them, it was mostly the tall skeleton that hung from the shelves.

Manny dared Janice to touch the skeleton. She refused, and Manny taunted, "Scaredy cat!"

"I'm not scared," Janice retorted.

"Liar, liar!"

Janice stomped up to the skeleton and prodded her finger into the bony wrist. It swung like crackling wind chimes. The kids screamed and dashed out of the room. Tales of the eerie lab room spread through middle school.

Although, by the time they were in their sophomore year, they knew the skeleton was just made of hard plastic. But it didn't stop the tradition of little kids tiptoeing through the building to confront the ghost that haunted the biology laboratory. While some were caught and chastised, the teachers didn't really stop them. It was way better for them to be interested than scared of it when having to learn about the skeletal system.

BEE IN YOUR BONNET

Nessie was so used to making tea in the morning that after decades of this, her husband forgot how to make it.

"Time to sharpen your brain," she clucked her tongue. "Go on. Two sugars, lots of milk for me."

John hobbled into the kitchen, ignoring a bee flying around his head. It took time to locate the tea. The sugar had disappeared. He didn't want to ask Nessie for it, so he got out the bottle of honey instead. Water boiling, he added the leaves and milk.

The rogue bee settled on the honey bottle. John snatched the bottle and shook it hard enough for his arm to hurt and the bee to disappear. He strained the tea into Nessie's favorite mug and added the honey. She would love this!

She didn't.

"Ugh! What's that taste?" Nessie shuddered.

"It's honey," he complained. "You hate honey now?"

Instead of answering, she dipped her spoon and brought out a drowned bee, its wings fluttering feebly.

Nessie gawked. "How much honey did you put in, John?"

STICKY SITUATION

Alfred fell asleep while he babysat his daughter's youngest child. He woke up to a wall full of Sharpie scribbles.

Lydia was proud of her art and eagerly showed her worried Baba her masterpiece. Alfred figured she was too young to understand the consequences, but he also didn't want Lydia's parents to come back to the mess.

So he did what any normal grandfather would and covered the lower wall with sticky notes.

Alfred tried to place Lydia in her playpen, but she managed to get out again and redraw her artwork on the sticky notes. By the time her parents come home, Alfred was exhausted, and Lydia was ecstatic.

"Wow, Dad!" Lydia's mom exclaimed, staring at the compendium of sticky notes. "You've been busy."

"I tried to stop her from marking the walls," he explained. "Didn't really work."

"No one's going to win that battle," Lydia's mom laughed. "We covered some of the walls with furniture when she began drawing, but it doesn't matter. Walls with marker doodles just mean there's a happy kid here."

BATTERIES

Most times hitting the TV remote enabled the channel to change. Other times, it needed batteries. Morgan found that out soon enough. He asked his wife, Iris, what else in the house needed new batteries.

"The dining room clock, your alarm, my watch, and your razor," Iris answered.

"Alright, I'm heading to the store."

Morgan bagged a parking spot in front of the store but had forgotten his walking stick. His knees would not thank him for it, so he was determined to walk slowly enough. Batteries for five things around the house. Ten single units, right? Wait, the watch had to have a smaller size battery?

He called Iris up. "What kind of battery do I get for everything?"

"Just the normal size."

"That would never fit in a watch!"

"Why do you need to buy a battery for the watch?" Iris asked, completely bemused.

Morgan spluttered. "You're the one who said it needs a new battery!"

"Yes, Morgan! You're supposed to take it to a watch shop and get them to fix it!" Iris said, exasperated.

SUGAR AND BACON

Reginald woke up one morning to find his ears blocked as though he'd flown a 14-hour flight. He wandered into the kitchen and heard his wife, Marion, say, "...bacon…today."

Bacon for breakfast? His favorite! She rarely pulled out the stops regarding greasy and fatty foods. They were watching their health, and treats like these were few.

"Excellent!" He cheered. "I'll get done with some papers and join you."

He volunteered at a local shelter and had some paperwork to complete. A sweet smell ensued from the kitchen, confusing him. Reginald returned to find Marion placing a tray of batter in the microwave. She turned it on and told him, "...ready…sugar…breakfast?"

Reginald stared. "You put sugar in the bacon? What's the batter for?"

Marion stared back. "Bacon…ears…wax?"

Reginald shook his ears, trying to dig his fingers in. They popped, and the noises flooded back in.

Marion snorted. "Breakfast is eggs and toast. I'm baking a cake for later, and we ran out of sugar. We should really get you hearing aids, Reginald!"

THE GIGGLE TRAIL

Claude's clicky pen, an old Parker, had been handed down to him by his father. He stepped out of the room to replace its refill. By the time he was back, the pen's body was MIA.

But he heard the sounds: click, click!

Someone had stolen it and couldn't help but press the end as they toddled off. Claude called out loud, "Fee, fie, fo, fen. Who's taken my clicky pen?"

Surely enough, his granddaughter burst into loud peels of laughter from the kitchen.

"Ellie? Is that you?"

"No!"

She dashed out from under the table and ran—or wobbled—to her room. Claude grinned and followed the baby at his leisurely pace.

And so, their afternoon passed, with Ellie giggling and clicking while Claude chased her around. When she fell silent, he checked behind the couch, and sure enough, Ellie was curled up there, sound asleep. Her new toy was clasped in her hand.

He picked her up, heading to her crib. "You'll have the pen one day, Ellie. For now, you can keep growing."

CHAPTER 5

LESSONS LEARNED

TRUST IN ME

The Thompsons had to sell their yacht. It was a 10-year-old sailboat that had worked well for a long time, especially before and just after Darla and Mani married.

But with a toddler hanging about and another baby on the way, they had to make allowances in their budget.

Mani exhaled. "Do you feel like we'd jumped in too quickly? We're pretty young with everything. Without the boat and then finding a bigger place for the four of us, how can you trust this would work?"

Darla smiled and embraced him. "I know it because you were so passionate about sailing; you spent months doing your research before even asking me about it. I know it because you still buy parenting books now, just in case there's some brand-new information. And it's also the same reason our baby laughs when you throw him in the air. He knows for sure you'll catch him."

She kissed him. "We trust you, Mani. So, trust me now. We're going to be okay."

POWER

Lisa's grandma ran the house with an iron fist. That being said, she was always fair with her judgment. When Lisa came home crying after her abysmal swim meet, where nobody encouraged her, her grandmother took her aside for a chat.

Instead of the usual lecture of "try and try again," Grandma soothed her and told her anecdotes about her younger days. Grandma was known in the neighborhood for her fierce voice. But what people hadn't known was she also liked slam poetry. She'd perform on soap boxes to passersby in the park because that was the only place she didn't get jeers from her audience.

Over the years, her motivation dwindled, and with it, her interest.

"Don't let others kill your passion," Grandma warned Lisa. "Nobody has the power to stop you from getting into the pool and washing the other racers away."

Lisa understood. Some months later, the inter-school swimming competition was held. Lisa won first place in the freestyle and broke the state record. The power to win had been within her all along.

PATIENCE

An airplane was delayed before takeoff. Air traffic control reported large swarms of birds in the airspace, so several planes were grounded.

The passengers sat in their seats for two hours. After a few minutes of silence, soft mutters and grumbling began. Then a baby cried. Conversations grew loud and dipped down like the ebb and flow of tides. The air circulation buzzed and sent a synthetic coolness to the passengers.

Yet, no one complained. There were no raised voices or arguments. Everyone managed to stay in their lanes and cope with the delay as much as possible. This let the air hosts get extra catering. We received more food and drinks than expected for the 50-minute trip.

The captain herself announced when the runways were open for business, and we sighed in relief. Perhaps the entire ordeal would've been less of a bother if the pilots hadn't played one song on repeat for the duration of the wait. It's a test of patience to be subjected to RHCP's Snow (Hey Oh) 25 times on a loop.

BOOK NOOK

José had several books in his home and was determined to turn them into a personal library. The minimum number of books that constituted a bonafide library was 100, including some restrictions. He was about 40 short of the number and embarked on a buying spree.

He toured the bookstores in and around his city. He visited stalls when he traveled and strove to purchase at least a couple of books in every place he explored.

When José hit the hundredth mark, he celebrated. He was a proud owner of his tiny collection of Critical Theory and American History volumes. People marveled at his tastes and perused them often. They commented on his well-read sensibilities and praised him for his dedication and patience. He'd gone above and beyond the requirement and showed no signs of stopping. José was titled a certified library owner; his collection having crossed more than 2000 unique volumes which covered multiple categories and genres.

Now, he just had to read them all.

THE BEST DIVORCE

Peter and Shantae divorced after six years of marriage. Everyone was stunned. They'd been high-school sweethearts who stuck together in a long-distance relationship all through college and who got jobs in the same city!

Shantae had tried to take Peter's bests with his worsts. She tried to reign in her temper and work on all the faults he'd brought up during couples counseling. Peter simultaneously worked on picking up after himself, doing more chores around the house, and managing his odd spending sprees.

They didn't have children, so it made things easier, but their family and friends protested. "Try to make a greater effort," "Maybe have a baby? Babies fix problems."

Divorce is taboo in many places, but people tend to forget it happens in bad marriages. Peter and Shantae were tired of hating this. They weren't giving up, just taking different ways out of a bad situation. After some months, both found meaning in life, in staying single and happy. It had been a tough journey, but they made it out intact.

SMART LUCK

Billy and Dalia were just eight, but they knew what was going on. Mama and Mom were arguing about grown-up stuff.

Claire found a great job post all the way on the other side of the country and was hired. Unfortunately, Alice didn't want to move. They'd be so far away from everyone in their lives. Claire was excited about full benefits, better insurance, and good schooling.

Alice retorted, "The chances of being able to save up enough money in a big city is like finding a four-leaf clover in the backyard!"

Dalia gasped. She whispered to Billy, and they ran out of the house. Alice and Claire were still debating when the kitchen door banged open, and two muddy children raced in. They proudly held out a hand full of four-clover leaves.

Billy chirped, "There were lots of three-leafed clovers. But we searched and searched and found these, Mama!"

Alice choked. Claire beamed, "Oh my! Good job, kids. I guess we can find good opportunities if we go searching for them."

CAMELIA'S TEETH: IV

Remember the milk teeth? One day, Camelia discovered matcha tea and could not get enough of it. After a month and a half of regular matcha, she was back in the dentist's chair with them checking her milk teeth, and wouldn't you know it? It was time to get them removed.

In her 20s, Camelia had an operation that lasted nearly three hours. It sounded a little tiring now, so they split it into sessions. To her surprise, her husband offered to wait for her in the clinic.

He'd brought earplugs so he wouldn't faint at any "untoward" sounds from the dentist's equipment. It was proof to her that people could learn and adapt at any age. She'd have to cut down on her matcha, and that would be unpleasant. But for now, knowing her husband was just twenty feet away, Camelia faced the anesthesia and drill with no fear.

HELPERS

Daisy turned 70 and found that she was now truly old. Her hair turned grey from the roots to the tips. She tracked the wrinkles on her skin all over. Her body had begun to sag while she descended into a funk.

Her husband, Trevor, sat in the rocking chair with her and said, “We lived this long with good health, darling. We have two wonderful dogs and an entire garden full of blooming life to show for it.”

Daisy sighed. “I’m being shallow.”

“You’re scared,” Trevor noticed. “What can I do?”

Daisy grimaced. “It’s not about what anyone can do. I’m just having a senior-life crisis.”

Trevor kissed her forehead. “I’ll always be here, darling. When your knees ache, I’ll rub a balm. When your feet hurt, I’ll massage them. And when you feel like this, we can stay in this rocking chair and watch the dogs play.”

Daisy cuddled up to him as the chair gently rocked. Some days weren’t the best, but with Trevor, she knew she’d be okay soon.

WINNER

Ruiwen was in eighth grade when she ran her first race. The intraschool sports competition was close, and her team practiced for weeks. One of the girls, Penny, wasn't all that fast, so the team placed her in the third position. Ruiwen was decent with the turns and was placed last.

At first, their team had gotten a good start. In the third round, Penny set off with the baton and lost the lead. Everyone groaned as she looped around and reached dead last, handing the baton over to the final runner, Ruiwen.

Ears burning, she ran, knowing there was no way to win now. The distance was just too much. Ruiwen could have just given up, and it might have made no difference.

But she put on a burst of speed and took the turns steeply, crossing the finish line just inches from the runner in front of her.

Ruiwen's team landed last, but she'd covered an incredible distance, catching up in record time. Pride bloomed in her, knowing she hadn't succumbed to failure.

PRIDE

Adam was retiring from an IT firm after 22 years. In his exit interview, Kathy from HR posed a few questions, which he answered uninterestedly.

Finally, she asked, "Is there anything you've learned in your last month?"

He thought it over. "Regardless of my decisions, this place will immediately replace me with a newbie or some automated program. My absence won't affect the environment in the slightest."

Kathy was surprised. "You're leaving because your job can be automated? Nobody can do your job in the exact way you do it. You bring a uniqueness to the office and your teammates in a way no AI program can. You led multiple projects, coached a lot of people, had lunch with them, and taught a lot of things over the years. AI can only be used to fulfill a productive role. Nobody can use you. You affected people."

Adam was stunned. That was true. The past couple of decades were fruitful. He hadn't lost anything during that time.

He was able to head out with his head high.

UNPARALLELED PARKER

Deborah used to be a valet driver and then a limo driver. Over the decades, she'd developed an incredible road sense. So, when her son asked her to pick up his car from the mechanic's, she agreed without qualms.

But it was a dense Freelander. After retiring some time back, she had her doubts about the big car, but he said, "You're an amazing driver, Mom! Give yourself some credit."

He sounded so sure that she obliged. Driving was straightforward. Parking was a hassle. Stuck in the narrow road between two cars, Deb stepped out and examined the tight space. Then, she flagged down a passerby to help guide her.

With the help, Deb managed to get into the spot neatly.

"Wow!" the passerby said wistfully. "I couldn't have parked it so easily. How'd you do it?"

Deb thought of her son, who believed in her so much he entrusted his beloved car to her care. "I have a lot of support."

RUN LIKE A GIRL

Simon had just moved to a new town and immediately announced he was a great runner. He boasted his timings to the other kids and challenged them, but nobody took him up on it. His new neighbor, Mathew, said, "How about you race my sister? Bonnie runs like a girl, but we'll see if you really are fast like you claim."

Simon placed third in his previous school. He didn't want them to know that! If anything, it would be nice to warm up. Mathew drew the lines, and Simon and Bonnie took their positions.

"Good luck," Bonnie winked, and when her brother whistled, the runners set off.

Except Bonnie dashed along the track leaving behind a dust trail. Simon reached the finish line second, absolutely blown away.

"But you said she was terrible!" he accused Mathew.

"No, Bonnie runs like all the other girls on her team," Mathew mentioned proudly. "You should see her medals!"

CAMELIA'S TEETH: V

"Is that chewing gum?" Camelia wondered, staring at the globs of green clay stuffed into a steel casing.

"No," the dentist laughed. "This isn't edible. We'll place it in your mouth, and you'll need to bite down to make sure your upper teeth and gums dig into it. Then we'll get another case for your lower jaw. The clay will harden, and we'll use it as a mold to make your dentures."

She nodded, feeling a little sad. Camelia and her teeth had been on a lot of adventures. She loved anything sweet, and her teeth would routinely pay the price for it (and she'd pay the price for them). And now, after decades of lattes, coffees, and drinks, her strong teeth were beginning to clock out.

"I can still have ice cream, can't I?" Camelia asked suddenly.

The dentist grinned. "In mediation. But yes, your remaining teeth are looking pretty solid. Just take care to use the mouthwash and floss daily."

She relaxed. As long as she could have her sweets, Camelia would be alright.

BOUQUET TOSS

Lanny's granddaughter was married in front of a hundred friends, and the wedding went without a hitch. When it came to the bouquet toss, Enid was shaking with unbridled energy. She practically flung her bouquet across the hall. Lanny caught it.

The party and the guests burst into laughter, and some of the young girls happily cheered Lanny on. But Lanny grimaced. She shouldn't be catching bridal bouquets meant for young ladies.

Enid approached her later and hugged her. Lanny tried to give the flowers back.

"No, Nana. You caught this. It's for you," Enid insisted.

Lanny sat back, unhappy. But Enid said, "It doesn't mean you have to find someone, Nana! It's just a pretty bouquet, a good icebreaker. You can just keep it in a vase, and no one will mind."

Huh. Traditions meant a lot, but if Lanny could avoid being stifled by them, then she could be doing something right. She went home with the flowers and safely placed them in a small vase where they stayed bloomed for a long time.

PERSPECTIVE

Amber never traveled. Her small-town life was pretty good, and she made do with what life gave her. But when her youngest nephew wrote one of his essays for college applications about her, she was blown away.

Luke called her sturdy. Instead of seeing her like a plant rooted to one spot all through her life, he saw her as a tree, growing stronger while helping others out. Her father's house had gone straight to her husband, skipping her, but Luke recognized that she was the one who truly made it a safe space and place to call home.

Everything Amber wasn't sure of or tried to ignore, Luke managed to turn into something positive or strong. He thought his aunt was a hard-working individual and not a monotonous busybody.

He wrote about her and sent it out to a university! There were people reading about Amber and realizing how much Luke admired her.

"And I used the same essay for a couple of other places, so now lots of people know," Luke said, grinning wildly.

FLOWER FORMAT

Patty redecorated her porch with bouquets. Bunches of flowers were hung from the ceiling, with gradient colors shifting from red to violet while passing through the rainbow spectrum. It lit up the porch, and Patty absolutely adored it.

Every week, she replaced the bouquets to avoid any wilting flowers. But that racked up the bill. As an alternative, Patty bought plastic flowers, just as bright and lovely to behold. She hung them all around the porch and tried to enjoy the sight, but it wasn't as fulfilling as she'd hoped.

Ethan came to the rescue. After 55 years of living with her, he knew exactly what to say.

"Hon, do you want the porch to just look pretty, or do you want real flowers?"

"Can't I have both?" Patty groaned.

"Sure," Ethan grinned, "Plant the flowers and keep them around the porch."

Less than a week later, Patty had proudly assembled an array of potted plants with saplings blooming. Having green solutions made things routinely better. The plants brightened up the porch and their lives.

ACAPELLA BURP

Estelle's house was filled with people humming, singing, rapping, and burping. Thanks to her husband, Roy, all their kids and grandkids used their musical talents to replicate an acapella group.

With family sitting in the living room and trying (and failing) to combine noises into a symphony, Estelle finally asked them what the point of it was.

"There's no point, my dear," Roy said. "We're just having fun."

The youngest kids giggled and began to show off the intensity of their burps. Estelle wondered how burping could be fun. Didn't that hurt their stomachs or their throats?

"You try, Nana!" the little kids cheered.

Nana smiled. "Thanks, sweetie. But I think I'll just listen. Are you composing a song?"

Roy laughed. "A grand composition by our very own orchestra! Hit it!"

At once, everyone burst into a cacophony of noises. Some sang their hearts out, and a few beat-boxed valiantly. Others rapped and burped along, and Estelle could not find a coherent tune other than the sheer joy that filled the house. It was amazing.

ADHD AT 80

There was a reason why Willy's shaving cream ran out so fast, why his cluttered house stayed that way, and why his to-do list lasted years. Willy's granddaughter pointed out his symptoms of attention-deficit hyperactive disorder.

He took great offense to that.

"You have the classic signs, Gramps," Melanie insisted. "You can hyperfocus but leave a lot of tasks incomplete. The shaving cream runs out because you shave a couple of times a day. It's such a routine thing; your brain just doesn't process it clearly. It's hard for you to clean up a desk, especially if you're used to the clutter."

"Next, you'll say I need meds," he groaned.

"Some medication can help you," she agreed.

"I just need to concentrate."

"You've been concentrating for decades," Melanie whispered. "Take a break, Gramps."

A break sounded wonderful. Learning about neurodivergence at the ripe age of 80 wasn't the worst thing in the world if Willy could ease up on himself. Whether or not Melanie was right, treating himself better was the key to a gentle life.

HEIRLOOM HANDOVER

When Connie passed down her diamond earrings to Elaine, it went smoothly. It was ten minutes of mother and daughter holding back tears as they examined Elaine's new countenance with the family's diamonds sparkling in her earlobes.

But two decades later, when Elaine tried to lovingly hand them over to Ivy, she refused.

"I'm not one for jewelry, Mom," Ivy said impatiently.

"This is a family heirloom!" Elaine spluttered. "It has always changed hands from mother to daughter."

Ivy didn't budge. Elaine called up her mother, and Connie practically exploded. "Those earrings belonged to my grandmother! It's always been in the family! Ivy has to wear them!"

Elaine groaned, but Ivy had other plans.

"Cole?" she called. "Do you want diamond earrings? They were Grandma's before she gave them to Mom."

Cole was ecstatic. "Are they really for me, Mom?"

Elaine hadn't seen him grin like that in months. Cole's grumpy exterior made the family call him the "emo cousin."

"Of course, honey!" Elaine said, her heart growing warm. "Family heirloom and all."

PAUL'S PH.D.

Paul achieved his doctorate when he was 90. He was a devout man, worked at the YMCA, and studied patterns of teenagers and their propensity to stress. He used years of knowledge to build his thesis on church work for the community. He spent three years on his research, during which he was able to put his expertise on life and career into his studies.

It was a memorable day when Paul was awarded his doctorate. His classmates, who were decades younger than him, included him in their circle and kept in contact for a long time. He and his wife, Joyce, were humanitarians and volunteered with NGOs and the community to help out those in need. They gave free education, taught classes, and coached anyone—from youngsters to business professionals—on the value of kindness and the joy of giving back to the people.

With his new degree in hand, Paul proved to everyone that you're never too old to learn new things in life, especially things that help others just as much as yourself.

THE THIRD SIDE

Gerald's colleagues threw a retirement bash for him, and he was glad.

"Thank you, all," Gerald nodded to the dozen people gathered in the faculty room. "This is a wonderful party. All I can say is as the years go by, the workload seems to increase without stopping, so here is my sole piece of advice. Draw your boundaries. You're not just educators preparing kids for the future; you're also people with real lives. Don't ignore that."

Some smiled politely, but a teacher said, "There's not much work-life balance for us, Gerald. You know this."

He nodded. "It's hard to find balance. But that's also like saying there are only two sides to a coin."

They stared. "Gerald, there are only two sides."

"Coins are three-dimensional objects," Gerald said. "No one really thinks about the rim because it's not useful for us. But without the third side, a coin is just a sheet of metal. Your time off is important to you. Don't ignore that side of you that needs rest at any point in your life."

PASSION

Hank found a new hobby when he was 72. He'd never thought much about magic tricks. But when he saw trick cards at a local variety store, he was intrigued.

He bought a full kit of things. It had fake coins he could bite or bend and strings that he could learn to knot and unknot. There were silver hoops and colorful scarves in the mix. He also located a manual that taught him how to distract his audience and perform a trick to dazzle them.

Prestidigitation became his passion. He loved to entertain his family with his simple tricks. It took several hours of repeated hand movements to make everything seem graceful and dazzling. He'd hide coins between his fingers and "pull" them out of his grandkids' ears. He'd cough and reveal a flower or cards bursting from his mouth. His quaint tricks were mere illusions, but there was nothing illusionary about everyone's delight.

Growing old felt incredible. Hank still had passion in his heart and the time to pursue something new, and so out of depth.

CONCLUSION

The best medicine is laughter, but for a balanced diet, we also need inspirational and light-hearted meals for the soul. These tales are packed with serene narratives, rib-tickling anecdotes, and creative chronicles, some of them even with a little twist to keep you warm and cozy.

Short Stories for Seniors is a compilation of earnest tales gathered from people who have found it cathartic and comforting to yield some of their experiences to the world. Have you found yourself in a similar situation as them? Perhaps you can see new meaning in certain escapades or discover how life tricks us into adventures when we let it.

P.S.

If you engage your friends and families with these accounts and become known as the Storyteller in your group, it's okay. We won't tattle!

REFERENCES

Canfield, J., & Hansen, M. V. (2009). *Teens talk growing up.* In A. Newmark (Ed.). Chicken Soup for the Soul Publishing LLC.

Finnemore, J. (2012, August 25). *John Finnemore - 50 things you must do before you're 30.* YouTube. https://www.youtube.com/watch?v=w2mO6KTrSrw

Goldstein, J. (2011, December 18). 102-year-old woman becomes the oldest skydiver in the world as she jumps out of plane for charity. *People.* https://people.com/human-interest/irene-oshea-oldest-skydiver-102-years-old/

India, T. C. (2017, March 27). *Meet Paul Siromoni, the man who earned a phd at the age of 90.* YourStory. https://yourstory.com/2017/03/paul-siromoni-ph-d

Nicksay D. & Platt M. (Producers), & Herman-Wurmfeld, C. (Director). (2003). *Legally blonde 2: red, white & blonde.* Type A Films; Marc Platt Productions; Metro-Goldwyn-Mayer.

Simmons, A. (2016, February 10). people shared their funniest family stories and it got heartwarming real fast. *Reader's Digest.* https://www.rd.com/article/funny-family-stories/

Printed in Great Britain
by Amazon